ROYAL COURT

The Royal Court Theatre presents

RED BUD

by **Brett Neveu**

First performance at the Royal Court Jerwood Theatre Upstairs, Sloane Square,
London on Thursday 21st October 2010.

D1092095

THE ENGLISH STAGE COMPANY
AT THE ROYAL COURT THEATRE

'For me the theatre is really a religion or way of life. You must decide what you feel the world is about and what you want to say about it, so that everything in the theatre you work in is saying the same thing … A theatre must have a recognisable attitude. It will have one, whether you like it or not.'

George Devine, first artistic director of the English Stage Company: notes for an unwritten book.

photo: Stephen Cummiskey

As Britain's leading national company dedicated to new work, the Royal Court Theatre produces new plays of the highest quality, working with writers from all backgrounds, and addressing the problems and possibilities of our time.

"The Royal Court has been at the centre of British cultural life for the past 50 years, an engine room for new writing and constantly transforming the theatrical culture." Stephen Daldry

Since its foundation in 1956, the Royal Court has presented premieres by almost every leading contemporary British playwright, from John Osborne's Look Back in Anger to Caryl Churchill's A Number and Tom Stoppard's Rock 'n' Roll. Just some of the other writers to have chosen the Royal Court to premiere their work include Edward Albee, John Arden, Richard Bean, Samuel Beckett, Edward Bond, Leo Butler, Jez Butterworth, Martin Crimp, Ariel Dorfman, Stella Feehily, Christopher Hampton, David Hare, Eugène Ionesco, Ann Jellicoe, Terry Johnson, Sarah Kane, David Mamet, Martin McDonagh, Conor McPherson, Joe Penhall, Lucy Prebble, Mark Ravenhill, Simon Stephens, Wole Soyinka, Polly Stenham, David Storey, Debbie Tucker Green, Arnold Wesker and Roy Williams.

"It is risky to miss a production there." Financial Times

In addition to its full-scale productions, the Royal Court also facilitates international work at a grass roots level, developing exchanges which bring young writers to Britain and sending British writers, actors and directors to work with artists around the world. The research and play development arm of the Royal Court Theatre, The Studio, finds the most exciting and diverse range of new voices in the UK. The Studio runs play-writing groups including the Young Writers Programme, Critical Mass for black, Asian and minority ethnic writers and the biennial Young Writers Festival. For further information, go to www.royalcourttheatre.com/ywp.

"Yes, the Royal Court is on a roll. Yes, Dominic Cooke has just the genius and kick that this venue needs… It's fist-bitingly exciting." Independent

ARTS COUNCIL ENGLAND

Supported by
ARTS COUNCIL ENGLAND

PROGRAMME SUPPORTERS

The Royal Court (English Stage Company Ltd) receives its principal funding from Arts Council England. It is also supported financially by a wide range of private companies, charitable and public bodies, and earns the remainder of its income from the box office and its own trading activities.

The Genesis Foundation supports the Royal Court's work with International Playwrights. Theatre Local is sponsored by Bloomberg. The Jerwood Charitable Foundation supports new plays by new playwrights through the Jerwood New Playwrights series. £10 Monday Nights is sponsored by French Wines: Wines of Quality. The Artistic Director's Chair is supported by a lead grant from The Peter Jay Sharp Foundation, contributing to the activities of the Artistic Director's office. Over the past ten years the BBC has supported the Gerald Chapman Fund for directors.

RED BUD

Brett Neveu

Characters

JASON COBBS
BILL RONFELDT
SHANE CUPPLES
GREG BOLLHOEFER
JEN BOLLHOEFER
JANA DAFFLITO

This text went to press before the end of rehearsals and so may differ slightly from the play as performed.

Early evening. Lights up on a shorn, dusty and overtrod campsite. A pickup truck, tailgate facing downstage, is parked near two dome tents, a wooden picnic table and an unlit fire ring. A number of folding camping chairs sit near the fire ring and three or four coolers rest in the shade of a spindly tree.

JASON COBBS, *dressed in jeans, tennis shoes and a T-shirt, enters. His right leg is on fire as he runs toward a plastic cooler.*

JASON. Ahhhghhh!

Tripping over the cooler, JASON *falls hard into the dirt. Entering quickly,* BILL RONFELDT, *wearing khaki shorts, a button-up long-sleeve shirt and tennis shoes, runs to his tent, opens the flap and grabs a small fire extinguisher. Rushing to* JASON, BILL *sprays the extinguisher on* JASON*'s leg.*

A pause. JASON *laughs.*

BILL. Your leg caught fire.

JASON (*laughing*). You don't think I realised?

BILL. Sure –

JASON. There was no goddamn need to spray me –

BILL. But your leg was on fire?

JASON. I was gonna dump water on it –

BILL. Still, but –

JASON. I was headed to putting it out!

BILL. You woulda got burnt –

JASON. I was hardly on fire! Jesus! I fucking cooler-jump that shit every year anyhow!

BILL. First year you ever caught fire, though. Gettin' a bit slow on the take.

JASON. No I ain't.

JASON checks over his pant leg. In the distance, a voice yells, 'Redbuuuuuuud!'

Just singed the pant leg. (*Beat.*) Redbuuuuuuud!

BILL. You gotta be careful, pants like those can go up like that. (*Snaps finger.*)

JASON. No they can't.

BILL. You never seen anybody's pants go up before and I have like a million times.

SHANE CUPPLES enters. He wears green cargo shorts, a button-up short-sleeved shirt and sandals. He sips a can of beer.

SHANE. Redbuuuuuuud!

JASON. Redbuuuuuuud!

SHANE. Your leg was on fire!

JASON. Oh damn, you know it!

SHANE. Shit! That's a fucking first!

JASON. I know, can you believe it? I was up in the air and then – smash, there I was right in the flames!

SHANE. If you weren't so fat you'd have cleared it –

JASON. Fuck off, I ain't fat –

SHANE. Damn Fireman Pete anyhow got you all fixed real quick. Fireman Pete sure is a good fire putter-outer.

JASON. Yeah – somebody should award Fireman Pete a big old Fireman Pete medal for saving the fuck out of my pants.

BILL. Jason's pants were on fire.

SHANE. And you put out the fire in his pants. You're a goddamn American hero.

A pause.

BILL. You guys seen Jana?

SHANE. What?

BILL. Jana –

SHANE. Seriously?

BILL. Seriously what?

JASON. That girl ditch you already?

SHANE. Probably ditched you right after you went to run and save Jason's goddamn pants.

JASON. Like every other girl you ever bring out here who ditches you.

BILL. I never got ditched out here before, that doesn't even make any sense.

SHANE. Makes more sense than you.

BILL. What?

SHANE. I said it makes more sense than *you*.

A beat. BILL *tosses the extinguisher back into the tent and exits.*

A pause.

JASON. You want a new beer?

SHANE. You know it.

JASON *crosses to one of the coolers and removes two cans of beer. Crossing back, he hands a can to* SHANE.

You were in that fucking fire.

JASON. Sure enough. (*Pause.*) Gonna be a hot one tonight I think.

SHANE. Always a hot one.

JASON. Not if it rains like it did those three other times like four years ago and nine years ago and fifteen years ago.

SHANE. It ain't gonna rain.

JASON. I'm sayin' it wouldn't be hot if it rained because of the rain. Anyhow, humidity is the problem, not the heat.

SHANE. 'It's not the heat – '

JASON. 'It's the humidity.'

SHANE. Don't matter to me whichever one, can't change the weather.

JASON. Yeah, just glad to be away from it all.

SHANE. What all you got to be away from?

JASON. You know, the pressures.

SHANE. What the fuck pressures you have?

JASON. Just 'cause I'm laid off don't mean things ain't pressured. Plus like your job is all that anyhow.

SHANE. It's something, which is more than you got.

JASON. Fucking secretary ain't much of something –

SHANE. I ain't a fucking secretary.

JASON. It's just Red Bud makes the pressure better, okay? It's the excitement.

SHANE. The Red Bud excitement?

JASON. It's always a fucking good time so yeah, *excitement*.

SHANE. Let me know if I ever say Red Bud's the most exciting thing in my life and I'll fucking kill myself.

JASON. I never said Red Bud was the most exciting thing in my life. It's just an exciting thing. In my life. Like every time we go. It's exciting. And fun. Every fucking time. It's exciting. (*Pause*.) What you think, that Bobby Wenthower, you think he might win it all tomorrow? Either him or Kevin Landish. Either one of those guys should take it this year. Either guy's got it. That's my opinion. Bobby or Kevin.

SHANE. Kevin won it last year.

JASON. He's the favourite.

SHANE. Gotta like the favourite.

JASON. You always like the favourite.

SHANE. And you always pick the asshole underdog.

JASON. I like the scrappers.

A pause. SHANE *pulls a pack of cigarettes from his pocket and lights up, then quickly re-pockets the pack.*

SHANE. Greg's late.

JASON. They probably hit the road late.

SHANE. Probably Jen waddling around the house getting ready takes fucking for ever. She's fucking huge.

JEN. She *is* fucking huge.

SHANE. Like – (*Gestures out from his stomach.*) fucking – bam.

JASON. Like one of those giant tuna they got in Japan.

SHANE. Like what?

JASON. Didn't you see that? The giant-ass tuna that sell for a cool million?

SHANE. You're fucking nuts.

JASON. Giant fucking tuna for giant fucking sushi. It's fucking true.

SHANE. Fucking Japanese.

JASON. I know, right? A cool million for some tuna when you can fucking get it in a can for like a buck. But damn if I had that Jap tuna, I'd have a fucking million bucks, swear to God.

SHANE. You gonna set up your tent some time?

JASON. I'm sleeping in the truck.

SHANE. In the bed?

JASON. In the cab.

SHANE. What?

JASON. Yeah.

SHANE. You're cramming yourself in the cab?

JASON. I sold the tent in the garage sale so I got to cram in the cab.

SHANE. What garage sale?

JASON. Like a month ago. At my mom's place.

SHANE. You never said you were havin' a garage sale.

JASON. Just sold mostly junk, that's all.

SHANE. What junk you sell?

JASON. Nothing, much. Just the tent and my sleeping bag. And my waterskis. Plus a bunch of CDs and DVDs. And some clothes. My computer. My camera. My stereo system. My waterbed. My mountain bike.

SHANE. That mountain bike was brand new.

JASON. Live a clutter-free life. That's what they say. It's about freedom. From clutter. So now I'm free. (*Pause.*) You want to play frisbee?

SHANE. Naw.

JASON. Remember that time we had those lawn darts and we were throwing them in the air and Bill got impaled with one right in the goddamn shin? (*Laughs.*) Shit, we gotta do that again this year –

SHANE. Check your phone.

JASON. My phone?

SHANE. Maybe Greg called.

JASON. You check your phone?

SHANE. Fuck my phone.

JASON pulls a cellphone from his pocket and checks it.

JASON. Don't have a signal.

SHANE. Let me see.

JASON hands SHANE his phone. SHANE looks at it then hands it back to SHANE.

JASON. You think Greg will ditch this year?

SHANE. No way.

JASON. 'Cause of Jen I wouldn't be surprised.

SHANE. He'd never ditch on this. Red Bud's an institution. You don't miss Red Bud.

JASON. The best time of your life?

SHANE. Yeah.

JASON. Shit, you're gonna have to kill yourself now you admitted it.

SHANE pretends to stab himself in the gut, hari-kiri style.

JASON and SHANE laugh.

Motorbike engines are heard from a distance.

We gonna wait for Greg all day or we gonna head to the qualifiers?

SHANE. We gotta wait.

JASON. But if he ditched –

SHANE. If the qualifiers are so important to you, then go.

JASON. I just want to go, go, go – you know?

SHANE. This is about relaxing, too.

JASON. Yeah, and the race.

SHANE. We'll catch the qualifiers, okay?

JASON. Sounds like they're revvin' up out on the track.

SHANE. If Greg ditched, we'll know soon, okay?

JASON. Yeah, all right.

SHANE. You fucking ass-monkey, calm down.

JASON. Redbuuuuuud!

From far off, a voice responds 'Redbuuuuud!'

Woo!

SHANE. Relax, okay?

JASON. If Greg don't come –

SHANE. He'll be here.

JASON. You're right. What am I worried about?

SHANE. Shit-all.

JASON. Let's sit back and relax, wait for Greg, and for the time being you and me will start the party to commiserating.

JASON *kicks back in one of the lawn chairs.*

It's time to party down!

SHANE. Fucking ass-monkey.

JASON. Let's par-tay! Yeah! It's time to party! (*Sing-song.*) Get up on your feet and par-tay! Par-tay!

JASON *climbs on the tailgate of the truck.*

SHANE. Time to par-tay?

JASON. Par-tay!

SHANE *joins* JASON *on the truck's trailgate.*

SHANE (*puts hand to ear*). Time to do what?

JASON. Par-tay!

SHANE *begins to dance.*

SHANE. To do whuh-whuh-what?

JASON. Par-tay, toot-toot! Par-tay, toot-toot!

JASON and SHANE *'party dance' and sing the 'party toot-toot' song.*

A pause. GREG BOLLHOEFER, *in shorts, T-shirt and tennis shoes, and* JEN BOLLHOEFER, *seven months pregnant and in clamdiggers, a button-up top and sandals, enter. They carry with them a duffle bag, a tent, a few camping chairs and a cooler. The two watch* SHANE *and* JASON *for a few moments.*

GREG. Somebody grab some of this shit.

JASON. Hey, Greg! You made it!

GREG. Why wouldn't I make it?

SHANE climbs down from the truck.

SHANE. Hey.

JASON. RED BUD! REDBUUUUUD!

GREG. Goddamnit somebody fucking grab something already.

JASON hops down from the truck.

JASON. Party time!

JASON and SHANE *grab a few things from* GREG. JEN *puts her things near the table.*

Where's your car?

GREG. They're doing one vehicle per site.

JASON. Aw hell, seriously? You shoulda called, we woulda drove down to pick you up, we coulda switched out with the truck if you wanted.

GREG. I did fucking call.

JASON. I got no signal, I guess.

GREG. Then that answers that.

JASON. Tomorrow after the race we'll throw your shit in my truck and we'll drive you back down to your car so you don't have to carry it to your car. Okay?

GREG. It doesn't matter, man.

JASON. Or I can put it on my back and haul it back like a donkey. (*Laughs*.)

GREG. Or stuff it up your ass like a fucking suppository. (*Laughs*.)

SHANE. With the size of Jason's ass, all that shit should fit just fine. (*Laughs*.)

All three men laugh.

GREG (*continues laughing*). Plenty of room, yeah.

JASON (*continues laughing*). Yeah, yeah, fuck off, fuckheads. (*Pause*.) Your motorbike back at the car?

GREG. We didn't bring the bike.

JASON. No motorbike?

JEN. Not this year.

JEN sits on a cooler and eats a bit of hotdog bun.

JASON. Because why?

JEN. Greg said he didn't want to.

JASON. How we supposed to get around later?

GREG. Who says we got to get around?

JASON. We always tool around on the bike after dark, plus you always bring the bike.

SHANE. Greg don't want to bring the bike then it's no big deal.

JASON. Twenty-two years and this is the first Red Bud with no bike.

SHANE. It ain't gonna kill us if there's no bike.

JASON. Yeah, okay.

SHANE. Don't worry about not bringing a bike.

GREG. I ain't worried about it.

JEN. How long you guys been here?

JASON. We already went walking around a bit, checked a few things out. They got a new pizza shack near the kid track and, like, a million new port-o-johns.

GREG. Where's Bill?

SHANE. Running around looking for his fucking date.

JEN. Who's his date this year?

JASON. Greg, listen to this –

SHANE. A skinny little thing.

JASON. She's fucking *nineteen*.

JEN. Nineteen?

JASON. Bill's totally doing a nineteen-year-old!

JEN. Seriously? She's nineteen?

JASON. She's just out of fucking high school.

GREG. Huh. Well. Good for Bill.

JASON. 'Good for Bill'?

GREG. Yeah. Somebody's gotta do a nineteen-year-old.

JEN. What's that supposed to mean?

GREG. Just that Bill is doing a nineteen-year-old.

JEN. And she's, what, a stable relationship?

GREG. No, just, it's something.

JEN. Something what?

GREG. Drop it, whatever.

JASON (*to* GREG). We got time before the qualifiers if you wanna start up something, maybe a quick Cooka King before we go.

SHANE. Greg don't wanna play Cooka King as soon as he gets here.

JASON. First thing's a sober-starting Cooka usually with everybody to send us off.

SHANE. We barely got time.

JASON. Just a quick game –

SHANE. Greg was late –

GREG. We had trouble getting going, that's all.

JEN. We gotta set up.

JEN *stands and begins unpacking some camping gear.*

SHANE. We can wait, it's cool.

JASON. Cooka King later then?

GREG. Yeah, okay.

JEN. Greg – grab the tent.

GREG *crosses to the tent bag and begins removing the tent.*

JASON. You want us to help?

JEN. Somebody should get the fire started. (*To* GREG.) Pull that post, Greg.

GREG. What?

JEN. Pull that post?

GREG. What post, what?

JEN. Pull that post through.

GREG. It'll pull apart.

JEN. No, just – don't jam it, just slide it.

GREG. It's gonna pull apart if I do that.

JEN. No it won't, just slide it.

GREG. It'll fucking pull apart.

SHANE. Here, hold on.

> SHANE *starts helping* GREG. JASON *joins in. The three men, working like a well-oiled machine, put the tent up in a flash. A pause.*

JEN. Somebody start the fire. Anybody get any wood yet?

> JEN *enters the tent.*

JASON. Maybe instead we could just pull some branches together or something instead of buying wood.

JEN. We're in an alfalfa field.

JASON. How about Shane goes and buys some wood?

SHANE. Grab a race schedule, too, when you buy wood.

JASON. You buy the wood.

SHANE. I'm not going the fuck anywhere –

JASON. Then give me some goddamn bucks for the wood.

SHANE. You got money.

JASON. I fucking drove you up here –

SHANE (*pulling out his wallet*). Here's fucking five bucks.

JASON. It's gonna be more than that.

> GREG *crosses to* JASON *and hands him a five-dollar bill.*

GREG. Here's five.

JASON. Cool. Thanks. Okay.

JEN (*semi-harsh, from inside tent*). Now go get some goddamn fucking wood!

JASON (*giving the men a look*). Jesus. Okay.

> *A beat.* JASON *exits.*

GREG *crosses to the cooler. As* JEN *exits the tent he removes two beers and a bottle of water. He hands the water to* JEN *and one of the beers to* SHANE. JEN *sits.*

GREG (*joking*). Sorry my wife's a bitch.

JEN. I'm tired from the pregnancy so I don't mean to be so, whatever, snappy. But you try being pregnant.

GREG. How would I go about doing that?

JEN (*to* SHANE). Next year Greg and me will be with the baby over in the family camp so this is the last year for doing it this way anyhow.

GREG. Doesn't mean next year will suck balls and doesn't mean this year will be shitty.

JEN. I'm not saying this year will be shitty or next year will suck balls.

GREG. How about we concentrate on having fun?

JEN. I am having fun.

GREG. And I'm tired anyhow.

JEN. After going to bed at eight-thirty last night?

GREG. I didn't go to bed at fucking eight-thirty.

JEN (*to* SHANE). Before even me, if you can believe it.

SHANE. Everybody gets tired.

JEN. More tired than a woman who's seven months pregnant?

SHANE. Sure. Fuck yeah.

GREG *opens a bag of potato chips.*

GREG. Who wants chips?

SHANE. Chip test?

GREG *shakes the bag.*

GREG. Chip test.

SHANE. What the hell flavour is it this year?

GREG. This year's fucked-up flavour is: (*Reading from bag.*) 'Salsa Super Cheddar Bacon Nacho'.

SHANE. Intriguing.

JEN. Last year it was 'Lemon-Lime Barbecue', right?

GREG. Yeah.

JEN. I liked those.

GREG. 'Salsa Super Cheddar Bacon Nacho'?

SHANE. Give me a few.

JEN. I'll try one.

> GREG *dumps some chips into* SHANE's *hand then into* JEN's *hand. They each do a taste-test.*

SHANE. It's cheddar-nacho-licious!

JEN. Pretty good.

GREG. Yeah, hey, pretty damn good.

> GREG, JEN *and* SHANE *dig in to the chips as* BILL, *black 'RED BUD' T-shirt in his hand, and* JANA DAFFLITO, *thin and wearing cut-off jean shorts, a hooded sweatshirt and sandals, enter.* BILL *and* JANA *hold each other close, arms around one another,* JANA *kissing* BILL's *neck.*

> GREG *stares at* BILL *and* JANA. BILL *notices the stare.*

BILL (*to* JANA). Jana, hey –

> JANA *demurely holds* BILL's *hand. The two cross toward the group.*

> What, you guys doin' the chip taste-off already? (*To* JANA.) Perfect timing!

> (*To* GREG.) What's the flavour?

> *A pause.*

GREG. 'Salsa Super Cheddar Bacon Nacho'.

BILL. Sounds awesome. Gimme some to try.

> GREG *hands* BILL *the bag of chips.* BILL *removes one and offers one to* JANA.

You want to try one?

JANA. No thanks.

BILL. C'mon, give it a try.

> BILL *eats the potato chip.* JANA *tries one.*

Tangy.

JANA (*mouth full*). Rwah.

> BILL *wipes the giggling* JANA*'s lips then hands the bag of chips back to* GREG.

JEN (*to* JANA). Hi, I'm Jen.

JANA. Hey.

BILL. Aw crap. Sorry. This is Jana.

JANA. Hey.

BILL. And that's Greg.

GREG. Hey.

JANA. Hi.

BILL (*gesturing toward* SHANE, *joking*). You already met this asshole.

> *As* BILL *steps toward* SHANE, *he accidently knocks over* SHANE*'s beer with his foot.*

SHANE. Fuck, damnit, Bill –

BILL. Oh shit – (*To* GREG.) You all running late?

GREG. Yeah.

BILL. I got Jana a T-shirt.

> BILL *holds up the T-shirt for all to see. The shirt is quite small and emblazoned with a giant, flame-covered motocross bike.*

Damn thing cost me like twenty-five bucks, if you can believe it. For a goddamn shirt. But it's the best one they had. Sexy, huh? (*Pause*.) Where's Jason?

GREG. Getting firewood.

BILL. Wow, Jen, you're huge.

JEN. Thanks a hell of a lot, Bill.

BILL. No, I mean, you're out to there with baby.

JEN. Stop describing my pregnancy as a giant shape.

BILL. Sure, sorry –

GREG. Enough, Bill.

BILL. You guys know what it is?

GREG. A boy.

BILL. A boy? That's great! A little Greg. Nice. A little, tiny Greg.

A pause.

GREG. Who wants a beer?

BILL (*to* JANA). You want a beer?

JANA. Yes.

BILL *crosses to one of the coolers and removes two beers. He opens both and hands one to* JANA. JANA, *smiling, takes the beer.*

BILL (*to* JANA). You wanna sit down?

JANA *sits in* BILL's *lap*.

Ow, my keys –

JANA. Oh, sorry –

A pause.

GREG (*to* JANA). You ever been to Red Bud before?

JANA. No.

In the distance, a voice shouts 'Redbuuuuuuud!'

BILL (*responding*). Redbuuuuuuud! (*Beat.*) This's her first time.

JANA. Redbuuuud!

SHANE. Redbuuuuud!

BILL (*to* JANA). Me, Greg and Shane and Jason have been comin' to this race since high school, no tents or anything back then. We'd just sleep in our clothes on blankets on the ground. Look up at the stars. Get high. Get drunk. Get wild.

SHANE. We get totally wild. As you can see.

BILL. True, that.

A beat.

JANA. Why?

SHANE. Why what?

JANA. Why did you start coming?

BILL. Greg got us started. He had a bike and was a hell of a rider –

SHANE. We came to hang and party.

BILL. It was the party aspect, too, sure, not just the race. It's a good time every summer out here for sure, a party and race combo. (*To* JANA.) Excuse me a sec, gonna put my keys in here –

BILL *slides out from under* JANA *and crosses to his tent.*

JANA. I been to stuff like this before, like a big outdoor concert.

BILL *puts his keys in his tent then crosses back to the group.*

SHANE. This ain't no outdoor concert, it's a fucking grand-national motorbike race that has huge implications on the race standings all over the fucking world.

JANA. At that outdoor concert we stayed up all fucking night. We were so wired from the music and the shit we were doing so we stayed up.

BILL. A good time had by all, I'm sure.

JANA. It was, it was a fucking party.

BILL. This thing's exactly that. A fucking party. With a grand-national motorbike race in the morning.

JANA. That's awesome.

BILL. I remember one of those nights back then, Greg there started a bonfire out of a roll of cyclone fence and he started tossing other shit into the fire like picnic tables and hotdog buns and fence posts. Then he rode his motocross bike around the fire, circling it and circling it, a burning shirt on a burning post raised above his head, in his hand above his head, him screaming 'RED BUD! RED BUD!' as that giant fire just got huger and huger. It was the hugest fire. Couldn't do a huge fire like that now, though. Get your ass kicked out doing that. Plus I'd feel like a hell of a hypocrite watching Greg make a huge fire and then somebody else coming and having to put it out.

JANA *stretches her hands out to* BILL.

SHANE. Fireman Pete can't let a fire just be a fire, he's got to be the one who puts it out.

BILL *grabs* JANA *by the hands and pulls her up. The two stand together and cuddle a bit.*

BILL (*to* GREG). They tell you about Jason cooler-jumping and landing in the fire?

JEN. He did what?

BILL. He nearly got seriously burnt.

JANA. Cooler-jumping?

JEN. No shit?

JANA *and* BILL *separate a bit, but continue to hold hands.*

BILL. That's when somebody rides a cooler down a slope, hits a jump and goes over a fire.

SHANE. First year he hit the fire. It was hilarious.

JANA. He jumped in a fire?

BILL. His pants hit the fire.

SHANE. Fireman Pete had an extinguisher in his tent and put out Jason's pants-fire lickety-split.

JEN. Holy shit! (*Laughs quite hard.*)

JANA. When was that?

BILL. Greg – where's your motorbike?

　A beat.

GREG. Didn't bring it.

BILL. You didn't bring it?

GREG. It was a hassle.

BILL. That doesn't make any sense. You just got that hitch last year and the thing slides right on –

GREG. I didn't bring the bike.

BILL. Well, shit. That blows. I was hoping to show Jana your bike. Maybe have her ride it. Fuck a duck. (*Long pause.*) We gonna head to the qualifiers in a bit, then?

SHANE. Soon as Jason gets back.

BILL (*to* JANA). The qualifiers are for to see who ends up in tomorrow morning's race.

JANA. That's what I thought.

BILL. We're thinkin' Kevin Landish –

SHANE. Bobby Wenthower –

BILL. Probably Dean Mickson, Russ Cane – Greg, who else?

　JANA *crosses to her beer, then sits.*

GREG. Um. Mike Dethoner?

SHANE. No way, fucking Mike Dethoner?

GREG. What the fuck do I know?

BILL. Anyway, the qualifiers, it's good stuff, a perfect chance to see what's what with the racers this year.

JANA. Sounds good.

BILL. The bikes get real loud and kick up a ton of mud. It's a hell of a show.

JANA. And maybe somebody will wipe out on his bike and get his arm fucking sliced off. Blood everywhere in the dirt or some really nasty shit.

GREG. Why do non-fans always want fucking wrecks?

JANA. Just thinking what shit could go down, is all.

GREG. Fucking blood on the track, that's what fucking people want to see. It's fucking sad.

BILL. I see her point, though.

GREG. I'm sure you do, Bill.

A pause. JASON enters. He carries with him a wrapped bundle of firewood.

JASON. Here we go. Fire-fucking-wood.

JASON tosses the wood on the ground.

BILL. Hey, all right, thanks. That's cool. Thanks, Jason. You need some dough? How much was it? Can I give you some cash?

JASON. Yeah. Ten bucks.

BILL hands JASON ten bucks.

SHANE. What the hell? Gimme that dough.

BILL. You pay for this?

SHANE takes the ten bucks.

SHANE. Greg – I owe you five. (*To* JASON.) You get a schedule?

JASON *removes a race schedule from his back pocket and hands it to* SHANE.

Thanks.

JASON. Yes, O Mighty Master.

JEN. How about some dinner then before we head to the qualifiers?

BILL. Sounds like a plan.

JEN. What, burgers okay?

BILL. You bet.

JEN. Everybody want burgers?

JASON. Yeah.

SHANE. Sure.

GREG. Mm.

BILL (*sliding up next to* JANA). Burgers okay?

JANA. Sounds good.

JEN. Where's the grill?

JASON. Aw fuck, the fucking grill.

JEN. You didn't bring the grill?

JASON. I sold it in the fucking garage sale.

JEN. What garage sale?

JASON. Just, I sold it and so I didn't bring it.

JEN. Why didn't you tell us you sold it before we came?

JASON. I got my mind full of other shit, okay?

JEN. We got a grill at home we coulda brought –

JASON. I don't got every second to think about a fucking grill.

SHANE. Don't turn this into something about Jen.

JASON. What?

SHANE. You see what you're doing?

JASON. What?

SHANE. Turning it into something about Jen instead of your fucking mistake?

JASON. I didn't see you asking about the grill –

SHANE. You're missing my point –

GREG. This ain't about anybody, okay? There's no grill so we'll figure it out.

JEN. Greg – run back to the car and grab the Coleman stove.

GREG. The Coleman's got hardly any surface area and plus it's just the burner and then the griddle. We'll just have to cook on the fire.

BILL. Yeah, let's just do some wieners over the fire with some sticks or hangers or whatever, like we used to. (*To* JANA.) That sound good?

JANA. Sure.

SHANE. Yeah, put your wiener on the fire, Bill.

JASON. Yeah, Bill. Jam your wiener on a stick and put your wiener on the fire.

SHANE *and* JASON *chuckle.* JANA *downs her beer.*

A pause.

BILL (*to* JANA). You need another beer?

JANA. Yes.

BILL *crosses to get* JANA *a beer.* BILL, *returning with the beer, plays a quick game of 'try and grab the beer from me' with* JANA.

JEN. Jana – how long you and Bill been together?

JANA. A week.

BILL. Just met her a week ago, yeah.

JANA (*playfully*). Gimme my beer, asshole.

> BILL, *smiling, hands* JANA *her beer.*

> So what's the draw?

JASON. For what?

JANA. The draw of this motorbike race?

JASON (*to* GREG). Women just don't get the draw.

JEN. That's a huge generalisation.

JANA. That's not what – I mean, I get the fast machines, the macho shit, but what's the *draw* draw.

JASON. What?

BILL. She means why do we come back every year.

SHANE. Is that what she means?

BILL (*to* JANA). The party and the race, like we said before.

JASON. It's exciting and fun and it's a getaway, that's why. That's the draw.

JANA. But every year?

GREG. A year's a long time.

JANA. So it's your tradition.

GREG. Yeah.

JANA. Cool.

GREG. Not everybody has to like it.

JANA. Didn't say I wouldn't like it.

GREG. But you don't have to like it because not everybody does. It's not for everybody.

BILL (*to* JANA). You better like it since I bought you that twenty-five-dollar shirt already. (*Laughs.*)

JANA. I'm just saying that if it were up to me I'd pick something the next year that had more whatever.

GREG. Meaning what?

JANA. Just, Jesus, more, you know.

GREG. I don't get what you mean.

JANA. You experience this.

GREG. Experience what?

JANA. And then you experience it. And. What, right?

GREG. What?

A pause.

JANA. Fuck what I'm saying. Never mind.

GREG. Say it again –

SHANE (*looking at the schedule*). The qualifiers start in twenty minutes.

JEN. Then somebody start the fire so we can eat. Hotdogs okay, then, with everybody?

JASON. Greg usually does the fire.

GREG (*to* JASON). You go ahead.

JASON. Me?

GREG. Yeah.

A beat.

JASON. Okay.

JASON grabs the bundle of wood.

(*To* GREG.) Borrow your knife to cut the bundle?

GREG. Yeah, here.

GREG digs a large pocketknife out of his front pocket and tosses the pocketknife to JASON.

JEN. Jason – where's your tent?

JASON. Oh, yeah – I'm sleepin' in the truck.

　　JASON *cuts the cord on the bundle of wood.*

JEN. In the back?

JASON. No, in the cab.

　　JASON *tosses the pocketknife back to* GREG.

JEN. Isn't it gonna be a little crammed in the cab?

JASON. I won't be crammed.

SHANE. He's just gonna jam his lard-ass right in there.

JASON. Fuck you, I've done it before.

SHANE. You have?

JASON. Yeah.

SHANE. When?

JASON. On the side of the highway just last week.

SHANE. On the side of the highway? Why were you sleeping on the side of the highway?

JASON. I was fucking tired, okay?

BILL. Why doesn't Jason just bunk with Shane in his tent?

SHANE. No way, it's a one-person tent, plus the dude kicks in his sleep.

JASON. I don't kick in my sleep.

SHANE. Back when he was in my tent in high school he fucking clocked me in his sleep right in the dick.

JASON. I'm sleepin' in my truck anyhow.

SHANE. You get your lard-ass stuck in that cab and Fireman Pete will have to run to his fucking firehouse for the jaws of life.

JASON. I'm not a fucking lard-ass!

SHANE. He'll have to yank him out, have those pincers get a tight hold of his lardy asscheeks and yoink!

JASON. I've had some fucking metabolism issues over the past year!

SHANE. Bah-boom bah-boom!

JASON. What the fuck is that?!

SHANE. You know – (*Walks like an elephant.*) Bah-boom bah boom!

JASON. Fuck you, I'm not some fucking pachyderm –

SHANE (*laughing*). 'Pachyderm'?

BILL. Shane, c'mon –

SHANE. Shut up, Bill, don't defend him – Jason knows he's a lard-ass.

JASON. Fuck you, Shane!

GREG. Who cares, Jesus, Shane, you're no better than him –

SHANE. 'No better'?

GREG (*laughing*). Yeah, Shane, you got a goddamn gut like fucking Buddha –

SHANE (*to* GREG). And what are you, Mr Fucking Muscle?

GREG. More fit than either of you lazy fucks.

BILL. It's just, whatever, all of us look fine considering –

JASON. Considering what?

BILL. Just that time takes a toll –

JASON. Coming from Fireman Pete, yeah, he's gotta be fit –

SHANE. That ain't true, half the guys at his firehouse weigh three hundred fucking pounds –

JASON. Just Fireman Pete here, he's gotta look like fucking Mr Fucking Muscle or some shit so he can get a piece of some nineteen-year-old pussy, am I right?

A pause.

BILL. That wasn't cool, Jason.

JANA. Don't worry about it, it's okay.

BILL. Jana's just not some piece of whatever.

JASON. I was making a point. Just fucking about Bill's fucking physique. (*Beat.*) No offense.

JANA. None taken.

BILL. I didn't hear you making the same fucking point to Greg –

JASON. To Greg?

BILL. About his wife –

JASON. What?

BILL. – and her age or whatever.

JASON. Greg's wife is the fucking same age as us and is already fat, so what sort of point would I have had to make?!

A pause.

JEN. I'm pregnant, asshole.

JASON. You know what I mean.

GREG. Jason.

JASON. Yeah?

GREG *grabs the bag of potato chips.*

GREG. You want to try a chip?

JASON. Chip test?

GREG. 'Salsa Super Cheddar Bacon Nacho'.

JASON. That's fucked up.

GREG. Try it and see what you think.

JASON. Here goes.

JASON tries a chip.

Not bad.

GREG. That's five votes in favour of this year's chip.

JASON. Five votes! This year's chip is a WINNER! (*Laughs.*)

SHANE. Gimme some of them.

GREG pours SHANE some chips.

BILL. We should get the fire going, huh? Maybe we can do the burgers on the Coleman and the hotdogs on the fire, that'd be good.

SHANE. We can all put our wieners on the fire.

A pause. JASON crosses to the firepit. He begins to ready the fire, making a tepee-shaped stack in the firepit with the logs and pieces of newspaper.

JEN. Greg – we still need the Coleman.

BILL. It's back in your car?

GREG. Yeah.

BILL. Jana and I can run and get it, you all want.

GREG. I'll get it.

BILL. We can go –

GREG. I'll go fucking get it myself in a minute so fucking relax, Bill.

JEN and GREG return to unpacking, removing buns and other food from bags and placing them on the picnic table.

JANA whispers to BILL, then peels away from him and enters their tent. BILL crosses to JASON, helping him with the fire.

JASON. I don't need your fucking help.

BILL. Just standing here, that's all.

A pause. JASON gets the fire started.

JASON. Whoosh!

BILL. Nice job, blob.

JASON. Fuck off. Greg – hey, look, check it out.

GREG. Good work.

JASON. I am THE GOD OF FIRE.

SHANE crosses to JASON and BILL.

SHANE. You guys know if Jen brought the stuff?

JASON. What?

SHANE. I'm asking if you know if Jen brought – 'the smoke'?

BILL (*smiling, to* JASON). The pot?

JASON (*smiling*). The 'pot'?

SHANE. Yeah.

JASON. Ask Greg.

BILL. She brought the usual container probably.

SHANE. Bill, you bring any?

BILL. No. Did you?

SHANE. That would suck if Jen didn't get some.

BILL. I'd ask Greg. (*Beat.*) Back in a second.

*BILL heads toward his tent and enters it. SHANE crosses to
JEN.*

SHANE. Greg – Jen bring the smoke?

JEN moves out of the tent a bit.

GREG (*slight smile*). The pot?

SHANE *looks toward* JEN. *A beat. From within* BILL'*s tent,* JANA *emits a girlish squeal. All look toward* BILL'*s tent for a moment.*

SHANE. Jen?

JEN. I brought some, yeah.

SHANE. Excellent. Thanks. Cool.

JEN. Yeah, especially since there's none for me.

SHANE. Right. Don't want a high baby.

JASON. Yeah. Fetal-marijuana syndrome. (*Laughs.*)

JANA, *emerging from the tent, now wears a bikini top.* BILL, *his hair a little mussed, exits the tent behind* JANA.

(*To* JANA.) Hey.

JANA. Hi, guy.

BILL. We gonna eat? Jana's gettin' hungry.

GREG *enters his tent.*

JEN. Yeah. In a bit.

BILL. Dogs on the fire, burgers on the Coleman, right?

JEN. Yeah.

SHANE. Jen's got the smoke.

BILL. Yeah? Cool, Jen.

JANA. 'The smoke'?

BILL. Pot.

JANA. Awesome, pot.

BILL (*to* JEN). You need any help with the condiments and whatnot?

JEN. No, I got it.

JANA. How about we get high before the hotdogs?

BILL. Before the hotdogs?

JANA. Anybody want to get high before the hotdogs?

SHANE. You mean now?

JANA. Yeah.

SHANE. Uh. Okay.

JASON. Me, too, yeah, sounds good.

JEN. We're getting ready to eat.

BILL (*to* JANA). Yeah, you said you were starving before anyhow.

JANA. But if everybody wants to get high then fuck the hotdogs. Let's get high.

JASON. Okay, then.

JANA. Redbuuuuud!

JASON. Redbuuuuud!

SHANE. Redbuuuuud! (*Beat.*) Circle toke!

GREG *emerges from the tent.*

JASON. Circle toke! Circle toke!

JASON *continues chanting 'Circle toke!' until he decides to stop.*

JANA. What's a circle toke?

JASON. You'll see, hold on –

GREG. So we're getting high first?

BILL. Guess we are.

SHANE. Great – so, Jen – grab the shit and let's light up.

JEN. So I'll just sit here while everybody gets high?

SHANE. That okay?

A pause. JEN *crosses to her tent, opens it and removes her purse. From within her purse* JEN *removes a small plastic container. She tosses the container to* SHANE.

Thanks.

JASON. Pipe's in the truck, hold on a sec.

JASON *runs to his truck and finds a small pot pipe.*

Here ya go.

JASON *hands the pipe to* SHANE. SHANE *sits in one of the lawn chairs and prepares the pipe.*

Pack it tight.

SHANE. Everybody sit down, relax, form a circle around the fire.

BILL. 'Circle toke.'

JANA. Ah, got it. Clever, clever.

JASON. Time to smoke-um Red Bud pipe! (*Laughs.*)

JANA, BILL, GREG *and* JASON *sit in chairs around the fire.* JEN *wanders toward the picnic table, grabs an apple, sits on the tailgate of the truck and begins eating.*

BILL. Maybe we do a couple of tokes then we all head over to the qualifiers, sound good?

JASON. So what do we play? Beer Names?

JANA. Beer Names?

BILL. Yeah, um, types of beer names –

JASON. Say a beer name then somebody goes next until we run out of beer names. Yeah? So. I'll say 'Budweiser'. So now, uh, Shane, you go next.

JANA. How about instead we play Shooters and Hits.

JASON. Shooters and Hits?

JANA. You know – Shooters and Hits.

JASON. So no Beer Names?

JANA *crosses to* BILL's *tent and digs around. From inside the tent she removes a large bottle of Jack Daniel's Whiskey.*

JANA. Shooters and Hits!

JASON. Shooters and Hits! I get it, yeah!

JANA. You all do Shooters and Hits, right?

SHANE. We do now. Pass the fucking bottle.

JANA *removes the top from the bottle and takes a swig, then passes the bottle to* SHANE.

There we go.

BILL. Good idea, Jana.

JANA. I know, right?

BILL *swats* JANA's *butt.* JANA *playfully knocks* BILL *in the side of the head.*

BILL (*half-joking*). Ow.

SHANE *takes a toke and a swig of the bottle then begins passing both. A long pause as the bottle and pot moves around the circle.*

JANA (*to* BILL). So now we just, whatever, chill and talk?

JANA *sits.*

JASON. Chill and talk?

BILL. Sure, okay, we can do that.

A beat.

JANA. So. Hey, everybody. What's up?

BILL. Red Bud, for one thing.

JANA. Right. (*Long pause.*) Jesus, okay, numbnuts fuckers, somebody ask me something.

SHANE. 'Numbnuts fuckers'?

JASON. Ask you something?

JANA. Just – c'mon, let's get rollin'.

JASON. What?

JANA. 'Get to know me', right?

BILL. Yeah, hey, you guys, get to know her.

A pause.

GREG. Jana –

JANA. Greg. Yes. Hello.

GREG. Hello.

JANA (*fake serious*). Yessir, what is your question?

GREG. Where you from?

JANA. Where am I from. I'm from just outside of Gary.

GREG. Where outside Gary?

JANA. Around the Colton area.

GREG. You grow up there?

JANA. Yep.

JASON. Where you work?

JANA. This shit is so boring to know!

JASON. Aw, c'mon –

JANA. Where do I fucking *work*? Jesus, you people – (*Laughs.*)

JASON. Bill – where's she work?

JANA. I work at the Casey's off of Highway 110.
Embarrassing, right?

JASON. They got pizza and sandwiches and everything at
Casey's, right?

JANA. You bet.

JASON. Like a fucking small-scale superstore. Pretty great.

GREG. How did you and Bill meet?

JANA. Ah. How did we meet?

GREG. Yeah. How did you meet.

JANA. Bill was at the Casey's filling up his car and came in to pay and he was all dirty from a fire and I thought that was sorta sexy.

JANA turns and tickles BILL. BILL *flinches, then playfully pushes* JANA's *hand away.*

JASON. No shit?

SHANE. Fireman Pete was sexy?

JANA. Why you call Bill 'Fireman Pete'?

SHANE. What?

JANA. He's a fireman, so then what?

JASON. It's his fucking nickname.

JANA. I don't think he likes it very much.

BILL. It doesn't bother me.

JANA. I can tell he doesn't like it.

BILL. Whatever.

JANA. It's like loser-boy playground shit.

JASON. No it's not. It's funny.

SHANE. Bill just said he don't mind.

JASON. It's funny and you know if you think dirt is sexy you will totally love Red Bud. The motorbikes run on a dirt track and the fucking dirt dust gets everywhere, all on your body like a fucking film of dirt. Sexy dirt all over the place here.

A beat.

BILL. You all ready to head to the qualifiers?

SHANE. We just sat down, Bill.

BILL. Didn't we all agree that was the plan?

SHANE. Fucking Fireman Pete –

BILL. What, we gonna skip the qualifiers now?

SHANE. Nobody agreed to any 'plan', so get your panties
    unbunched.

BILL. Fuck you, you fucking slug.

SHANE. What?

BILL. You're a fucking turtle without a shell, you motherfucker.

SHANE. A turtle without a what?

BILL. Just, Jesus – !

SHANE. What the fuck are you fucking yelling about, dipshit?

BILL. You're a fucking invertebrate!

GREG. Bill –

BILL. Fuck him, Greg, okay? He's a fucking invertebrate
    dipshit!

GREG. Shane's not a fucking dipshit.

BILL. All I want is to have a good time and avoid this tense
    fucking shit!

GREG. Nothing's tense, Bill.

BILL. Then fine. Fuck it.

GREG. Settle down.

SHANE. Fuck Bill anyhow.

GREG. Shane, Jesus.

    BILL *takes a toke on the pipe and a swig of Jack Daniel's.*

BILL. Just, whatever, I just want to fucking look at the stars in
    the sky and shut my fucking eyes and not be so fucking
    tense. (*Long pause.*) Sorry if I made everything weird. But
    shit. C'mon.

A long pause. BILL *stands and walks away from the circle a bit.*

JANA. Greg – where do you and Jen live?

GREG. In the city. Near the corner of Western and Clyborn.

JANA. What you all do for a job?

GREG. Jen teaches grade school. I do factory work.

JANA. What factory?

BILL. Hellson Manufacturing on the south side.

JANA. What does the factory make?

BILL. He makes polyurethane belts.

JANA (*to* SHANE *and* JASON). And what about you guys?

JASON. Shane's a secretary.

SHANE. I'm not a fucking secretary.

JASON. Right. (*Laughs.*)

SHANE. And Jason's out of work. (*Laughs.*)

JASON. I'm not out of work, I got fucking laid off.

SHANE. From a lawn-chemical company.

JEN. Jason, you remember that woman who worked there?

JASON. Which woman?

JEN. You know, that one woman –

JASON (*laughing*). Oh God, that one?

JEN. Yeah –

JEN *crosses toward the circle.*

That woman who smoked like she was a fucking living bonfire, she sat next to that vat –

JASON. Oh yeah! (*To* JANA.) At that place where I worked there was this big vat of fertiliser about ten feet from this woman's desk – the vat where the guys there would fill up our chem containers in the mornings and all that shit, those fumes, stunk to high heaven. Maybe that's why she smoked.

JEN. But the woman –

JASON. The woman, she was like sixty or something but she looked at least eighty because she looked so shitty and she sat there smoking and smoking day after day and so this one time I said to her, 'Your goddamn hair and clothes must smell like absolute shit when you get home.'

JEN. And the woman, she was like –

JASON. This fucked-up old woman, she just stared at me, her eyes all bloodshot, her skin all grey, her hair all limp and weird, her dried-up lips hanging open with that whatever Winston or Capri Slim whatever smoke was sticking out from her shrivelled-up, wrinkled fingers –

JEN. – and she didn't say a fucking word!

JASON. *Not a fucking word.*

JEN. She just sat there staring at him!

JASON. I thought she musta been a goddamn zombie! Some shitty old bitch zombie!

JEN. And Jason was like, 'She's gonna eat my brains, she's a goddamn dead fucking zombie!'

JASON. 'SHE'S GONNA EAT MY FUCKING BRAINS!'

JEN *and* JASON *laugh their heads off.*

JANA. Then what happened?

JASON. Then what what?

JANA. Was the woman okay?

JASON. Was she okay what?

BILL. Jana means did the woman ever get sick or –

JASON. Did she what?

BILL. Ever get sick or –

JASON. I don't know, shit –

JANA. You just made her sound so shitty I thought there was more to the story.

JASON. The point of the story was that she was shitty.

JEN. The point of the story is the woman was like a fucking zombie.

JANA. Yeah, but –

JEN. I guess, I mean it was her whatever realisation that her life was shit after Jason said what he said and it sorta struck her like that and stunned her into whatever zombie thing she ended up being.

JASON. Exactly.

    SHANE *lights up a cigarette, then quickly pockets his pack.*

BILL. I think what Jana's asking –

SHANE. Let her talk for herself, Bill.

BILL. What?

SHANE. I think Jana's the one who's the expert on what she's asking.

BILL. Excuse me for translating. It's just I know how you assholes think.

JEN. I'm an asshole?

BILL. Just –

JEN. And you know how I think?

BILL. I'm just trying to facilitate –

JEN. Why are you trying to 'facilitate'?

BILL. Because I get Jana's point –

JEN. Being what?

BILL. That, so, you guys, you know, with that story, I mean, the woman was sitting there and fuck, I lost my train of thought so fucking thanks. Jesus.

JANA. I was only saying I thought there might have been more to the story, like what happened to her after you saw her every day after that or something, like a moral or whatever.

JEN. There isn't a moral. That was the whole story.

JASON. Besides that woman, hell even with that woman, she wasn't all bad, besides her I liked that place, the hours were good and the work was just spraying weeds. That shit ain't hard.

SHANE. It was a pathetic place to work. Admit it.

JASON. Wasn't either.

SHANE. Sure it was.

JASON (*to* JANA). Shane killed a kid.

JANA. Shane did what?

JASON. You want a story with a moral, there's a story with a moral –

SHANE. Jason –

JASON (*to* SHANE). That thing with the electrical transformer. That's why you're a fucking secretary.

SHANE. That's not why I'm a secretary.

JASON. Yes it is.

SHANE. I didn't kill a kid, ass-monkey.

JASON. Yeah, you did.

SHANE (*to* JANA). I work for the Department of Human Services in Cicero.

JASON. As a secretary. Since you killed that kid.

SHANE. Shut the hell up, Jason!

JASON. Tell her –

SHANE. Jesus –

JANA. Yeah, tell me.

SHANE. I didn't kill a kid.

JANA. Then who killed a kid?

JASON. Go on, tell it.

SHANE. It's just – I used to be a caseworker and there was this kid –

JASON. This kid was playing –

SHANE. Fucking – Jason? Just let me – okay? (*Pause*.) There was this kid and he was playing in his backyard with his friends, running around with some other kids, running into each other's yard –

JANA. How old was the kid?

SHANE. He was little. Just six or a little older. The kid was electrocuted. The kid was running and jumped over a fence onto one of those electrical transformer boxes and for some reason the box was sending jolts out and when he stepped on the transformer box, he was killed. The shock threw him twenty feet. And then this lady, the mother, my office found out she'd been going to work and leaving the kid on his own and the kid was skipping school and that's when the kid was electrocuted on the transformer.

BILL *moves behind* JANA, *hugging her shoulders a little*.

JANA. The kid died?

SHANE. Yeah. The kid died.

JANA. Fuck, that's awful.

JASON. So they busted Shane down to secretary.

JANA. Why?

SHANE. The kid was sorta part of one of my cases. And I was
completely keeping track of the family, doing my job, making
sure the mom wasn't neglecting the kid. And then the kid
went out on his own and got killed on that transformer.

JASON. Shane was all distraught and shit.

SHANE. Fuck you.

JASON. Shane was distraught like 'Oh Jesus!'

SHANE. Wouldn't anybody be fucking distraught?

JASON. Shoulda never let it happen in the first place then you
woulda never been distraught.

SHANE. I'm gonna fucking slit your fucking throat in your
sleep and then you'll see whether or not I'm distraught.

JASON (*laughing*). You're gonna slit my fucking throat?

SHANE. Fucking ear to goddamn fucking ear.

BILL. No need for fucking talk like that.

A beat. BILL *sits.*

JANA. You ever see anybody dead?

SHANE. What?

JANA. Like a dead body someplace? You ever see that?

JASON. How we get on this topic?

JANA. From the dead kid. (*Beat.*) So none of you ever been
asked that before?

JASON. Why the hell would anybody get asked that?

GREG. Let's not do this morbid shit.

JEN. No fucking kidding.

JANA. It's not morbid.

GREG. Maybe that shit's interesting to you but it's fucking
morbid, okay?

BILL. It ain't too morbid.

GREG. Fuck if it isn't.

BILL. I've seen plenty of dead people and that's just how it goes.

JANA. That's where I was going with the question.

BILL. Exactly.

JANA. I was gonna say that the world is full of more dead stuff than alive stuff and that's the point.

SHANE. That's what your point was to what?

JANA. So I'm saying, Shane – don't feel bad about that kid. Life is long but death is longer, right?

JEN (*to* JANA). What are you doing here?

JANA. What?

JEN. Is this fun for you?

JANA. This?

BILL. Of course it's fun.

JANA. The reason I'm here is because Bill asked me and I thought Red Bud would be a kick, so yeah, it's fun.

JEN. You have any interest in the race?

JANA. Why, you have interest in the race?

JEN. Of course I do.

BILL (*to* JANA). You'll like it once you get out there next to the track. It sorta sweeps you in. For the uninitiated, it can look like who knows what. But once you start watching, the excitement takes hold of you and those bikes going flying through the air, it's pretty incredible.

JASON. Greg probably wishes he could be out there, too, probably wishes it was ten, fifteen years ago and he could jump out there.

GREG. I don't wish that.

JANA. Were you a racer, Greg?

JASON. Yeah, Greg, I bet you wish you could show everybody some goddamn moves and shit.

GREG. I don't wanna show anybody any moves.

BILL. Greg wasn't professional but he liked to ride all the time, did it on the weekends. We'd follow him up to the track, line up by the fence and watch him pull up on those hills and he'd turn his fucking wheel mid-air like a goddamn pro, ride high up on the seat and give us a salute as he took the air. He was a goddamn spectacle. It was fucking amazing. (*To* GREG.) Should have brought your goddamn bike, you know?

   A beat.

GREG. I didn't bring the bike, so what.

JASON. It's not a big deal.

SHANE. Yeah, fuck it, Bill.

BILL. Is Greg pretending he didn't used to ride or something? (*To* JANA.) Greg was hell on wheels on his bike back twenty years ago.

GREG. Shut the fuck up, Bill.

JANA (*to* GREG). You must be excited for the race tomorrow.

GREG. What?

JANA. The race. You must be excited to watch. Since you were hell on wheels.

JASON. Bobby Wenthower's gonna rock tomorrow, that's for sure.

BILL. Kevin Landish is the one who will take it.

SHANE. See? Bill says Kevin Landish, too.

JASON. Kevin got that messed-up shoulder, four, five weeks ago –

SHANE. Kevin's still the favourite to win.

BILL. With that messed-up shoulder things'll be tough for him, though, Jason's right.

JASON. Flexibility issues.

SHANE. That shoulder's fine by now.

BILL. Come tomorrow, ridin' down off those two big hills in that last leg, not to mention La Rocco's leap's gonna be tough for Kevin, it's true.

GREG. If it were up to me, I'd say fuck those hills and just hit 'em hard, consequences be damned. I'd visualise the fucker and pull up hard every time, using the goddamn lift to bring me up and home. Kevin Landish's upper-arm strength is for shit. I'd pull up and mow 'em down.

JASON. Shit yeah.

GREG. It's about power when you're on those hills.

JANA. You'd be the one who knows, right?

BILL. Greg would be, yeah.

JEN. We gonna head to the qualifiers, then, some time?

GREG. I'm fine sitting here, there's no need to go.

JEN. I'd like to see at least some of the qualifiers.

GREG. I'm fine here.

BILL. I'd be up for seeing some of the qualifiers.

GREG. We're staying here.

JASON. So, what, we're gonna skip the qualifiers, then?

GREG. Fuck the qualifiers.

JANA. I'm fine stayin' put if folks want to.

BILL. All right, sure. Let's stay. (*Beat*.) Should we start the hotdogs maybe?

JANA. I'm not really very hungry just yet.

BILL. We can hold off with dinner for now if everybody wants to.

JANA. Mind if we hold off?

BILL. Not at all.

JANA (*to* SHANE). Can I get a cigarette?

SHANE. Uh. Sure.

SHANE gives JANA a cigarette and lights it for her. He then lights one up for himself.

JEN. So, what, we're stayin' put and not having dogs?

JANA. That's the plan, right?

BILL. Sure.

JEN. Then what?

BILL. Whatever, right?

A pause.

JEN. Wonderful. Fine. Let's sit on our asses.

GREG. Jen.

JEN. Greg.

GREG. Stop *fucking bitching for, like, two seconds*!

A pause.

JEN. What?

GREG. Fucking you heard me.

JEN. Fucking *what*?

GREG. Fucking you heard me! Stop fucking bitching!

JEN. I'm not *bitching*.

GREG. Then what would you call it?

JEN. Expressing my human displeasure at the situation.

GREG. 'The situation'?

JEN. We're just gonna sit here?

GREG. Try keeping your displeasure to yourself.

JEN. It's not like I'm fucking screaming at somebody.

GREG. You can't let this be what it is!

JEN. Screaming.

GREG. You can't let this be some fucking bubble, some moon or some shit, some planet out on the edge of some shit and let that other shit just live back on Earth, just let it drop and we'll fucking give it a rest and fucking be on some other fucking planet. Why can't we give the bitching or whatever 'displea- sure' a *goddamn fucking break* and let this fucking planet be?!

A pause.

JEN. How would you like me to respond to that?

GREG. By doing just what I said. Let this planet *be*. Let it drift along in its own fucking universe.

A pause.

JANA. Sometimes at the Casey's, you know, sometimes I'm in there real late and nobody's come in for, like, hours and I start to lose my vision in the candy racks, all the colours bleed into each other, all the reds and yellows and oranges start to bleed and with those fucked-up overhead lights everything turns blue and bright and I start to think, 'Hell, am I in the universe? Am I, like, a planet in the universe? Am I not Jana any more but instead am I a planet circling some far-off star and all this shit, all the candy bars and magazines and pizza and beer is, like, space debris or asteroids and I'm like an inhabited planet out there in space going along for millions of years and only now am I coming to the realisation of who and what I am? Am I only now drawing those lines, making those connections right now and it's taken me this long to figure it out? Am I only now doing that *right now*?'

SHANE. Everybody has those feelings.

JANA. Yeah?

SHANE. People feeling like they're small. (*Beat.*) I remember I got a telescope when I was a kid and I looked at the moon through it and I thought to myself, when I got a good close-up of it, I thought, 'Damn, look at the size of the moon.' And the moon is sitting up there and huge and I'm sitting down here and I'm just a speck of tiny dust.

BILL. I never feel like I'm small and everything else is big. I sometimes feel like everything is small and I wonder what stuff is actually big.

JASON. I sometimes feel like shit is small and big at the same time.

JANA. Sometimes it feels like all of it, like the universe could turn all inside out and swallow you whole.

JASON. Like reverse something?

JANA. Yeah, like something switched and then you're all flipped inside.

JASON. Like its opposite?

JANA. Like black is white and white is black and whatever.

SHANE. The stars, their light, it's millions of years old before it hits us on Earth.

JANA. Everybody knows that.

SHANE. But, okay, right now, *experience* it. Experience that old fucking light coming down at you. Light that first was lit a million years ago and just now, you here just now, that's it finally hitting you and if you weren't here then that shit wouldn't have happened.

JANA. Time is a fucking wild ride.

BILL (*to* GREG). What do you think of that, huh, Greg? You think time is a fucking wild ride?

GREG. Everybody's gonna die eventually anyway so time don't fucking really matter, does it?

JANA. Who's the morbid one now, am I right?

GREG. Down the line, we're all dead. (*Pointing at each member of the group*.) Me, you, him, him, him, her – (*Pointing at* JEN's *abdomen*.) him inside there –

JEN. Nice.

GREG. That kid'll live whatever fucking life and is gonna die, too, it's just facts.

JEN. Great.

GREG. Time don't stop for babies.

JEN. He gets to be born –

GREG. He don't need to be born to know he's gonna die.

JEN. Jesus Christ, where's this from?

GREG. Just, you know, it's just conversation.

JEN. Your fucking shit turned on a dime.

GREG. It fucking didn't, it's just fucking conversation, Jen.

JEN. Conversation isn't saying shit about how your fucking baby's gonna some day die...! That's not fucking conversation...!

 A pause.

JASON. How about we play Cooka King and liven this shit up?

BILL. Cooka King!

JANA. 'Cooka King'? What's 'Cooka King'?

 A pause. SHANE *quickly puts a beer can on top of his head.*

JASON. Shit –

 GREG *puts a beer can on top of his head, as does* BILL.

 You assholes.

SHANE. Drink.

JASON. Damnit.

JANA. A fucking drinking game! Awesome!

SHANE *searches the campsite for a long stick.*

BILL. Drink, Jason. (*To* JANA.) He's last with the beer-top, so Jason drinks.

JANA. This is the game?

BILL. Yeah. This is the game.

A beat. JASON *grabs a beer and drinks it down.*

JASON. REDBUUUUUUUD!

SHANE. Second beer-top at start of Cooka was Greg.

BILL (*to* JANA). So now because of that, Greg gets to be Cooka King.

SHANE *hands the stick to* GREG. *A pause.*

GREG. Can check.

JASON *turns his can over. A bit of beer drips out of the can.*

JASON. Shit.

SHANE. Arm out.

JASON *puts his arm out.*

JANA. What the fuck is 'arm out'?

BILL. Jason didn't finish his beer, so –

GREG *smacks* JASON*'s arm with the stick.*

JASON. Ow.

JANA. Jesus. Hardcore.

JASON. Didn't hurt, really.

GREG *hands the stick to* JASON.

BILL (*to* JANA). So now Jason's the Cooka King with that.

JASON. See if Greg woulda really pounded me then now's my
   chance to get revenge if I want.

SHANE. Jen, you playin'? You can use water or whatever.

   JEN *puts a beer on top of her head.*

JEN. One beer ain't gonna hurt nobody.

JASON. Yeah? Okay. All in!

BILL. All in!

JANA. Now what?

BILL. We keep going. (*Beat.*) You better beer-top, Jana.

JANA. Oh, fuck.

   JANA *puts a beer on top of her head.*

BILL. Jana's in.

JEN. Okay – proclamation, Jason.

BILL. King's choice, go.

JASON. Cooka challenge.

BILL. Cooka challenge!

   JASON *points the stick at* SHANE.

JASON. Two tokes and the rest of your beer.

BILL (*to* JANA). Challenge goes to Shane.

SHANE. That's the challenge?

JASON. That's the challenge.

SHANE. Not much of a task.

   SHANE *gestures for the pot pipe. Whoever has the pipe
   hands it over.*

   Where's the pot?

   JEN *tosses* SHANE *the container of pot.*

   Thanks.

JASON. Go for it.

SHANE *does two tokes and downs the rest of his beer.*

SHANE. Done.

JASON. Redbuuuuuud!

SHANE. Redbuuuuuud!

JANA *and* BILL. Redbuuuuuuud!

JANA *and* BILL *sloppily make out for a quick moment.*

JASON. Can check!

SHANE *starts to turn over his beer can as* JANA *grabs the stick from* JASON.

What the fuck, hey –

JANA. Cooka King!

JASON. You're not supposed to grab it!

SHANE. Grabbing rule, she's King.

JASON. What?

BILL. Grabbing rule, he's right. From, whatever, ten years ago.

JASON. 'Grabbing rule'? Shit, really?

JEN. Just let her do it.

A beat.

JASON. Fucking fine.

JANA (*to* JASON). I decree you shut the hell up.

JASON (*covers mouth*). Muh-mmm-hum!

JANA *laughs.*

JANA. No, you can totally talk, seriously, sorry –

JASON (*removing hand*). Blah blah blah – (*Laughs.*)

JANA *laughs.*

BILL (*to* JANA). You gotta do a challenge.

JANA. That's right.

JEN. Make it a good one –

JANA. On who?

BILL. Anybody.

JANA. Um, uh – (*Pointing stick.*) Shane?

SHANE. Oh shit, again?

JANA. Oh right, forget it – um, Greg?

BILL. Greg's up!

JANA. Okay. Greg. You have to, uh – (*To* BILL.) does it have to be about drinking?

BILL. Usually it is –

JANA. Then, Greg – finish the Jack.

GREG. Finish the Jack?

JANA. It's not like there's a ton.

JASON. Cooka King has spoken! Finish the Jack!

JANA *grabs the bottle of Jack Daniel's and holds it out to* GREG.

JANA. Drink up!

GREG. Fuck me, okay.

GREG *takes the bottle and downs the rest of the whiskey.*

REDBUUUUUD!

All answer GREG *back with a strong 'Redbuuuud!'*

JANA. Bottle check!

GREG *up-ends the bottle. The bottle is empty. All cheer.*

GREG (*putting out his hand*). Stick.

JANA *grandly hands* GREG *the stick.*

JEN. King request!

BILL (*to* JANA). That means Jen's got a suggestion –

GREG. Go ahead.

JEN. Beer shot. Beer shot for, uh, Jason.

JASON. I'd do a beer shot.

JANA. Like what, 'beer shot' –

JASON. Shotgunning.

JANA. Oh yeah, perfect! Shotgun!

JEN. Decree it!

GREG. Jason must shotgun a beer.

BILL. Cooka challenge!

JASON. I gotta shoot it, huh?

GREG. Guess so, yeah.

> BILL *grabs a beer as* GREG *tosses him the pocketknife.* BILL *pops a hole in the base of the beer can with the pocketknife, tosses the knife on the table, then hands the can to* JASON. *Covering the hole with his mouth, he quickly tips his head back and pulls the tab on the can. The beer slams into his mouth.* JASON *gags. All cheer.*

JASON. Holy fucking Christ.

JEN. Can check.

> JASON *up-ends his beer. A slight amount pours out.*

> Ooo – arm out!

JASON. Damnit –

GREG. Feels like déjà vu.

> JASON *puts his arm out.* GREG *winds up to strike, then barely touches* JASON.

JASON. Ow.

GREG *tosses* JASON *the stick.*

JANA *quickly puts her beer can on her head.* GREG *does the same, as does* JASON, BILL *and* SHANE. JEN *comes in last.*

JEN. Fuck.

JASON. Jen – last on the beer-top!

JEN. I was, I was.

A beat.

GREG. Let's make it an all-play.

GREG *gives everybody a beer.*

JASON. Okay.

SHANE. Sure.

BILL. I'm in.

GREG. All-play!

The group downs their beers. A pause.

BILL. Jana, first on the beer-top from before, you're King.

JASON *reluctantly hands* JANA *the stick.*

JANA. Awesome. Okay. Uh – can check!

BILL, JASON, GREG *and* JEN *all turn their cans upside down.*

BILL (*to* JANA). Turn over your can.

JANA. Right –

JANA *quickly turns over her can. The beer can is empty.*

JASON. Shane –

SHANE *turns over his can. Beer pours out.*

SHANE. Shit.

JANA. Yay! Arm out!

SHANE *puts his arm out.* JANA *hits* SHANE *with violent force.*

SHANE. Ow motherfucker!

SHANE *backs away from the group.*

Fucking cunt! You fucking broke the fucking skin!

JANA. Ugh, sorry?

BILL. Relax, Shane.

SHANE. God*damnit*!

A pause.

BILL. You bleeding, Shane?

SHANE. Yeah, I'm fucking bleeding!

BILL *grabs a few napkins and crosses to* SHANE.

BILL. Here, use these, put some pressure on it.

SHANE. Get the fuck away from me.

BILL. Just thought you were fucking hurt, Jesus.

SHANE. Ow fuck! (*Beat.*) Fuck! (*Pause.*) Okay. Give me the fucking stick.

BILL. C'mon, Shane, it was an accident.

SHANE. 'An accident'?

BILL. C'mon –

SHANE. Give me the stick.

BILL. Don't fucking do that.

SHANE. Do what?

BILL. Who doesn't eventually get hit hard anyhow?

SHANE. It's my turn with the stick.

BILL. She doesn't have to give you the stick.

JANA. What do I care if he has the damn thing?

> JANA *throws the stick at* SHANE. SHANE *picks it up and points it at* JANA.

BILL. Shane, seriously?

SHANE. It's the game, right?

BILL. You're gonna fucking hit Jana with a stick?

SHANE. Only if she can't do the challenge.

BILL. You're not gonna hit Jana.

SHANE. If she don't do the challenge then she gets hit.

BILL. She don't get hit, challenge or not.

SHANE. Yeah, she does.

BILL. You ain't hitting Jana.

SHANE. I'm gonna fucking hit her.

BILL. Then I'll rip your fucking guts out. Plain as that.

> *A pause.*

GREG. Shane.

SHANE. What, Greg?

GREG. How about me instead?

SHANE. What for?

GREG. I'll take the challenge, do me instead.

> *A pause.* SHANE *points the stick at* GREG.

SHANE. Fine. That please everybody?

GREG. What's the challenge?

SHANE. Fuck. Uh. The challenge… is three beers.

GREG. Three beers. Fine.

SHANE. You gotta down three.

JEN. You're gonna make him puke.

GREG. I'll do three. No problem. Get me three beers, somebody.

JASON *grabs three beers from the cooler.*

JASON. Three beers is the challenge.

GREG *takes the three beers. He begins to drink one then starts to gag.*

GREG *stops drinking and puts the beers on the table.*

SHANE. No can check needed, I don't think.

GREG. Sure.

SHANE. Okay. Put your arm out.

GREG. Fuck my arm. Try my face.

SHANE. Do what?

GREG. Hit me in the goddamn face instead.

SHANE. What for?

GREG. My choice, isn't it?

SHANE. No.

GREG. Fucking hit me in the face.

SHANE. No fucking way.

GREG. Hit me in the fucking face!

SHANE. I'm not hitting you in the fucking face!

GREG. Fucking hit me in the goddamn fucking –

SHANE *strikes* GREG *in the face with the stick.* GREG *falls to the side. A pause.* GREG *stands, holding his bleeding cheek with his hand.*

BILL. You all right?

GREG. Yeah.

SHANE. Jesus – I'm fucking sorry.

JEN. Greg –

GREG *stares at the blood on his hand.*

BILL. Maybe it's time we head to the qualifiers –

SHANE. The qualifiers are pretty much *fucking over*, Bill.

BILL. Or maybe we could just fucking walk around, I don't know, clear our fucking brains, enough of Cooka King, right?

JEN. Maybe we should eat.

GREG (*looks at his hand*). Blood.

GREG *shows the bloody hand to the group.*

JEN. Jesus, Greg, get a napkin.

GREG. Life is exploding, it's pouring out of me. Fucking life is pouring out.

JEN *grabs a napkin from the picnic table and moves to wipe GREG's hand.*

(*Pulling away.*) Stop it.

JEN (*holding out the napkin*). Here, clean up.

GREG. No.

JEN. Wipe it off.

GREG. No.

GREG *takes a step back and stares at the group. A long pause.*

Something happened.

JEN. Something happened, yeah, you got hit with a stick.

SHANE. I'm really fucking sorry, Greg.

GREG. I did something at work.

JEN. You did something at work?

JASON. What are you taking about?

GREG. I pissed on a machine.

JEN. You pissed on a machine?

GREG. I pissed on a machine at work.

JEN. When did you piss on a machine?

GREG. Two days ago. I went behind this machine, this trash thing, this compactor for waste. I was walking the floor and I squeezed behind the machine and turned and pissed on it. The machine right away shorted out and something on the inside of it caught fire and then it all caught fire. I was back there, I'd jammed myself back in there, I was smelling the wires and melting plastic and fucking metal and my own fucking burning piss and I was like – 'My fate is fucking sealed. That this could be an okay way to go out.' My fucking burned body all melted with that machine, with the metal and wires and the concrete, with the components and the smoke going up to the ceiling, that it would be an okay way to die. But then this big asshole security guy got to me and reached around and pulled me out and took me outside, put me in the fucking grass. And I guess the fire wasn't much of anything, a couple of maintenance guys got it out with two fire extinguishers. I told my boss I spilled a soda. That it was an accident. But fuck I would have loved to have died back there.

BILL. Trust me, Greg, you don't want to burn up like that.

GREG. Seemed like the best thing, to burn up back there with the machine.

BILL. Believe me, it isn't.

GREG. Let that fire burn me up, let myself get eaten by flames.

BILL. That's not what happens to somebody on fire.

GREG. A quiet pile of ash and smoke.

A pause.

JASON. That's fucking *messed up*.

SHANE. You mean it's pretty much fucking insanely hilarious.

JASON. It is! You're right! (*Begins to laugh.*)

SHANE. Pissing right on a fucking machine like fucking *pissssss* – !

    SHANE *mimes* GREG *urinating on the machine.*

JASON. Then catching on fire like, 'Uh-oh I'm on fucking fire!'

    SHANE *mimes catching silently on fire.* JASON *laughs even harder.* SHANE *joins him. Both laugh like banshees.*

GREG. Jason and Shane. Jason and Shane. Jason and Shane.

    SHANE *and* JASON*'s laughter fades.*

    Shitheads.

JASON. What?

GREG. You shitheads are fucking deadweight.

JASON. Deadweight?

SHANE. What?

GREG. Both of you are dead-fucking-weight dragging every-body who's near you's shit into the fucking terminal void.

JASON. Meaning what?

GREG. You're fucking deadweight and I can't stand the fucking sight of your faces.

JASON (*approaching* GREG). Okay, hold on –

GREG. Don't –

JASON. What?

GREG. I said… don't!

    GREG *sucker-punches* JASON *in the face.* JASON *hits the ground hard.*

    (*To* JASON.) You don't even fucking come near me ever again.

BILL. Goddamnit, what the fuck, Greg?!

> BILL *begins to cross toward* GREG. SHANE *gives* BILL *a shove back.*

SHANE. Back the fuck off, Bill.

> SHANE *helps the bloodied* JASON *off the ground.*

JASON (*getting up*). Yeah, Bill, Jesus, back the fuck off.

BILL. C'mon –

JASON. Fucking shut up, Bill.

BILL. Greg fucking –

SHANE. Kiss my fucking ass!

JASON. You're not on fucking fireman duty, okay?!

BILL (*to* JASON). Greg fucking sucker-punched you –

JASON. So what? Who cares? Who really gives a shit? You fucking give a shit? Who the fuck are *you*? Fucking Fireman fucking Pete, running around putting out shit when nobody asked you to, fucking putting out my fucking pants-fire, fucking jumping up and waving your arms, nobody asked you to fucking wave your fucking arms, Bill. Nobody ever fucking asked!

BILL. Wave my fucking arms?

JASON. You like pants-fires so much, then here –

> JASON *grabs* BILL *by the arm and tries to pull him into the fire.*

BILL. What the hell are you doing – ?

JASON. Burn your own fucking pants –!

> BILL *struggles with* JASON *and smacks him in the side of the head.* SHANE *quickly grabs a burning log from the fire and whacks* BILL *in the back of the skull with it.* BILL, *quickly unconscious, falls to the floor like a cut tree.*
>
> *A pause.*

JANA. Holy shit, dude.

GREG *crosses to the fallen* BILL *and begins to take a long, heavy piss all over him.*

Shit.

JEN *moves toward* GREG *and tries to knock him away from* BILL.

JEN. Oh my God stop doing that!

JANA. Fucking shit –

GREG *pushes* JEN *back and continues pissing.* JEN *tries shoving* GREG *once more and* GREG *pushes her yet again, this time much harder.* JEN, *incensed, quickly grabs the pocketknife from the table and points it at* GREG.

JEN. Stop!

GREG, *looking at the pocketknife, stops pissing.*

Stop doing that!

GREG *zips up.*

GREG. I did stop.

JEN. Fucking stop.

GREG. I stopped.

JEN. Fucking stop.

BILL *begins to come to.* GREG *quick-reaches toward* JEN *and pulls the knife from her hand.*

Oh God.

GREG *points the knife at* JEN.

Greg –

GREG *turns the blade of the pocketknife to his own throat. A pause.*

JASON. Greg –

JEN. Greg –

GREG. I remember –

BILL. Jesus, Greg –

SHANE. Greg, Jesus –

GREG. I remember one time, long ago, I was on my bike and I was out on a farm, some farm and it was the middle of autumn and the leaves were spinning around and I was pulling my bike full-throttle, readying myself for a few jumps but going down this new blacktop road full-throttle and it was so beautiful, the air, the sun, the wind – all so beautiful and this is what I was thinking, this is what was in my mind: nothing. There was nothing. My head was just air. My mind was all white. My thoughts were just clouds. There was nothing in my head but road and leaves and wind and sunshine. Nothing but nothing. That was oblivion. And now oblivion is my gift to myself. And my gift to you. So. Let's enjoy it. Let's cherish it. This oblivion we are about to receive. Let's take it all in completely, our entire bodies wrapped in its bright, able light. Let's embrace my oblivion... together.

His hand steady, GREG holds the blade tightly to his throat. A very long pause.

GREG, *relenting, lowers the pocketknife.*

GREG *drops the pocketknife to the ground. A beat.*

GREG *slowly exits.*

A pause.

JANA *quickly walks to BILL's tent and grabs her bag, then begins to exit the opposite direction to GREG.*

BILL. Jana, wait – c'mon, don't leave, Jana, please don't –

JANA *looks at BILL for a moment. BILL begins to stand, his hand stretched to JANA.*

Everything is fine.

BILL *then groggily crumbles back to the ground, wincing as he falls.*

A pause.

JANA *exits.* BILL *watches after her. A pause.*

Fuck.

JEN *crosses to the picnic table and sits.* SHANE *moves toward a lawn chair, sits, and stares into the fire.* JASON *crosses near his truck and sits heavily on the tailgate.*

Damnit.

JASON *cups his hands to his mouth.*

JASON. Redbuuuuud!

JASON *lowers his hands.*

A pause.

In the distance, a lone voice shouts 'Redbuuuuuud!'

A beat.

Blackout.

The End.

A Nick Hern Book

Red Bud first published in Great Britain as a paperback original in 2010 by
Nick Hern Books Limited, 14 Larden Road, London W3 7ST, in association with
the Royal Court Theatre, London

Red Bud copyright © 2010 Brett Neveu

Brett Neveu has asserted his right to be identified as the author of this work

Cover image: Pietari Posti
Cover design: Ned Hoste, 2H

Typeset by Nick Hern Books, London
Printed and bound in Great Britain by CPI Bookmarque, Croydon, Surrey

A CIP catalogue record for this book is available from the British Library

ISBN 978 1 84842 135 6